PARAGRAPHS

The Wesleyan Poetry Program: Volume 91

VERN RUTSALA

PARAGRAPHS

WESLEYAN UNIVERSITY PRESS

Middletown, Connecticut

Grateful acknowledgment is made to the following magazines, in which some of these poems have appeared: *Quarterly Review of Literature, Stand, Kayak, December, The Seventies, The Iowa Review, Seneca Review, The Application, The Dragonfly, The St. Andrews Review, Equal Time, Pebble, Millmountain Review, Happiness Holding Tank, Poetry Now*. Special thanks are due to The Best Cellar Press for *The Harmful State*, a pamphlet containing twelve *Paragraphs*.

Library of Congress Cataloging in Publication Data

Rutsala, Vern.
    Paragraphs.

    (The Wesleyan poetry program ; 91)
    I. Title.
PS3568.U83P3   811'.5'4   77-20145
ISBN 0-8195-2091-8
ISBN 0-8195-1091-2

Manufactured in the United States of America
First edition

To Joan

CONTENTS

On Paragraphs 15

It Is the Same Today 19

Upstairs 20

Lunchroom 21

Late at Night 22

My Dancer 23

The Rules of the Dead 24

Underwater 25

Faces 26

Reasons 27

Advice 28

Sirens 29

Diet 30

The Embarrassed 31

Infants 32

Guilt 33

Summer 34

The Ghost on the Second Floor 35

Golf 36

Joy Joy   37
Charles Burchfield   38
The Public Lecture   39
Why I Wrote on Sidewalks   40
Houses & Ships   41
Bodies   42
These People   43
Professors   44
On Being Nervous   45
Free   46
Settling Down   47
Culture   48
Heroes!   49
The Lonely Man   50
The Lonely Man Speaks   51
The Lonely Man Writes   52
The Affliction   53
We   54
The Orthodoxy of Routine   55
Dream Reel   56
Demon   57
Friday at 4:30   58
Conference   59

O Tannenbaum   60

The Art of the Woodcut   61

Things   62

Killing Time   63

The Visitor   64

The Talent Hunt   65

Signature   66

Double   67

Missing   68

Report on the Day   69

Cave   70

They   71

Friends   72

Ego Lives Alone   73

A Gathering   74

Killers   75

The Harmful State   76

Are you genuine? Or merely an actor?
A representative? Or that which is
represented? In the end, perhaps you
are merely a copy of an actor ...
— NIETZSCHE

Experience is one of the forms of pa-
ralysis.
— ERIK SATIE

Urgent action is not in graciousness
it is not in clocks it is not in water
wheels. It is the same so essentially,
it is a worry a real worry.
— GERTRUDE STEIN

A soldier had had both arms blown
off in combat. His colonel offered
him a gold piece. The soldier replied:
I suppose you think, Sir, that I've
only lost a pair of gloves.
— MAX ERNST

A man must swallow a toad every
morning if he wishes to be sure of
finding nothing still more disgusting
before the day is over.
— CHAMFORT

PARAGRAPHS

ON PARAGRAPHS

The Paragraph is a prose poem, but it is also related to the fable, the aphorism, the maxim, the character, and the joke, and may draw energy from the ghosts of those forms in the way free verse is said to rely on the hint of traditional meter.

*

Occasionally a Paragraph will read like a parody of an aphorism. This is purposely done. They are supposed to be poems rather than chips of wisdom, but they do play with expectations – the appetites that exist for the "inspirational," "living thoughts," box-of-chocolates kind of knowledge that so many people secretly admire.

*

One of the primary technical problems of the Paragraphs was the creation of something like the plastic artist's illuminating shift of materials. (Oldenburg's ghost typewriter, for example.) One way of doing this was simply to use an assertion. Another was to employ the "right" tone. A further and more complicated way was that of so structuring the sentence that assurance was arrived at with apparent ease and naturalness, the realization accomplished, as it were, before the reader was aware of it because of the inevitable demands and expectations of conventional syntax. With luck the effect is essentially metaphorical in that, frequently, an object is made to seem to change its nature radically while continuing to bear its usual associations. Whatever apparent distortions occur have to be close to reality as in all metaphor, of course. An arbitrary switching around of objects is valueless: something about a lunchroom must suggest an arena.

The rhythm had to remain the rhythm of prose in which the phrase has weight but only within the context of the sentence, just as, in turn, the sentence exists within the overall structure of the paragraph. When a Paragraph began to fall into "lines" it failed, and any conventional poetic heightening struck a false note immediately. The surface had to be calm, even dry, in order to allow the event to break through.

*

Form: How to move from A to B quietly but inevitably, "incontrovertibly," while also strongly suggesting that the destination is actually C *and* D *or* E.

*

Form: The hope was to make an artistic entity, a block of words sewn together in many ways, and free of the random, notebook-entry quality so many prose poems have. Though in writing the Paragraphs any "established" short prose form interested me as a potential model: notebook or diary entries, thank-you notes, memos, answers to quiz questions, etc. Sometimes, of course, such forms are parodied though parody is rarely the primary aim.

*

A problem: How to make the Paragraph outrageous or absurd with a straight face.

*

Another problem: How to make something like poetry rise from the explicit, even dull statement. If this can be managed anything is possible.

*

Writing paragraphs—something considerably more than fillers—used to be one of the legitimate jobs on a newspaper. It was a craft, and crafts should not be allowed to die out.

*

Surely notes were made while the Paragraphs were being written. But they're upstairs, in the murk of old journals which now seem like collections of dust and shadows, impossible to penetrate. Furthermore, I'm not sure who wrote them.

*

Most of our "models" are bad, heroes who embody weaknesses, who become advocates of particular infirmities. To be like them you must make yourself sick. The problem is to use language well enough to prevent you from thinking this sickness is health.

*

You should be careful about making claims. Before you know it you'll be wandering around skid row begging for a grubstake and with that in hand be compelled to work your claim to the exclusion of all others, until its vein and yours become hopelessly intertwined.

*

One of the constants within the sequence is a quiet parody of official prose of various kinds—interoffice memos, readers' reports, political pronouncements, or that peculiar prose often elicited by notes on your own work.

IT IS THE SAME TODAY

I sit in the soft chair, or something very like me sits there, smoking and watching. They come in: the creature of effacement, all but invisible; the typographical error who is never corrected; then, a whole flock of shrugs and winces, closer together and more interdependent than bricks. There are eyes, hands, pimples, coffee—each creature like a simple declarative sentence repeated day after day.

UPSTAIRS

Downstairs doors open and slam. The house shivers with heavy feet going back and forth, crosshatching paths on the rug. Another door slams. A window quakes in its frame. This is the sound of panic. An entire herd shies at thunder and heads for the cliff, but the great ghostly stallion, mane flying, saves them at the last instant, himself falling, tail braiding and unbraiding in mid-air, and when he hits, the calm water in the deep gorge turns white forever. Yet he rises, spits on the branding iron, and heads for the mountains, upstairs.

LUNCHROOM

The knives on the table are there for a purpose, but their true function has been forgotten over the years. Actually, the lunchroom which now appears so calm and civilized is an arena, the trays and tables converted shields, and we who sit so quietly are gladiators. The man who cleans up, the one who looks so dull, grew tired of the mess and has cleverly diverted us by serving food to slice and eat, thereby satisfying our need to use weapons, which he stealthily reduced in size until they now seem innocuous, just as he has assuaged our desire to kill by teaching us the rudiments of gossip.

LATE AT NIGHT

Not willing to exert the mind enough even to sense the quality of the lives of those nearest us, we will, however, late at night, create from scratch around a few random sounds in the cellar—pipes knocking, the furnace working—a whole human being, the prowler come to punish us for lack of love.

MY DANCER

My dancer stands still most of the time—like an anchor. In fact, his feet leave the ground only when he hoists himself into bed. Your dancer may spin and jump. My dancer sneers and says, "I hate sweat!" His background? Close-order drill at Fort Benning, trick knees, poor wind. Here are a few of his dances: The Dance of Spilled Milk and Burned Food; The Morris Chair Polka; The Tango of the Coffee Urn; The Linen Closet Schottische; and, his masterpiece, The Coma Mazurka.

THE RULES OF THE DEAD

When young we see them and say, "Why, they're only pretending. Stay long enough and you'll see an eyelid flutter." But we are impatient and move on. Time gets shorter and still no one has told us the rules one must follow in order to appear, but not be, dead.

UNDERWATER

Our days are warm, without any sensation but drifting. The people we meet are distant, as if hidden within the soft armor of whales and porpoises. We dimly sense them, shadows swimming by; their concerns, their perceptions, their complex lives clenched inside those smooth bodies. No one touches. No one even looks.

FACES

There is our daily quota of faces: rows of them arranged neatly for ready reference, but they're all written — "fervently penned" — by administrations and The State. Some are illegible, blurs, discarded sketches, smudged chalk drawings. Others are like doodles on memo pads, obscure marginalia, graffiti. A lot are first drafts, a few say DRAW ME — simple clean lines and Orphan Annie eyes. Once in a great while on a back street you see an old man bent over to conceal his origin in the notebooks of Leonardo da Vinci.

REASONS

You ask what was wrong? Why did you talk that way? I have no answers. It was morning, summer, the newspaper lay spread like a map on the table. It sent me in odd directions. I had to say something.

ADVICE

A long day full of conflicting and abrasive impressions automatically produces agitation. Back home you move around restlessly, trying to cancel the mistakes you made and wincing with embarrassment. This happens every day yet you continue to work as you always have, just as you continue to despise your uneasiness. You fail to realize that agitation is your particular addiction, a thing necessary for your well-being.

SIRENS

Just now they moaned as they always do. They are in pain when someone presses the button which is for them like the exposed nerve in a bad tooth. So they scream until the pressure stops and allows them to sink back to what they like best: silence, moisture beading on their lips, darkness.

DIET

A single encounter with an acquaintance in a week, a few moments of conversation about the weather, provides enough of doubt, worry, irritability and melancholy to last for a season since each shrug, glance, inflection, and nuance is permeated with meanings we cannot understand. In the face of this it is amazing that people spend whole days together filled with hours of conversation. It is as if at a dinner each person were served entire schools of baked fish and herds of roast beef.

THE EMBARRASSED

You see a woman you know, and unaccountably, you become embarrassed. You stammer and can't wait to get away. It is only later that you remember: yes, last night you were together—in your dream. The next time you see her you look closely, eagerly seeking some hint of embarrassment in her actions.

INFANTS

Many speak of the looks of wisdom infants have but there is another quality rarely mentioned: the melancholy amusement in their eyes. This look arises from resignation, which, in turn, results from the infant's uncanny politeness, a politeness profound as sacrifice. Faced with an existence of possibilities without limits, the chance to be a lamp post or an ode or an inland sea, the infant, with infinite compassion for his parents and a deep understanding of compromise, more or less agrees to become a child.

GUILT

We sense a criticism, possibly overhearing it as we walk, and immediately we begin rearranging our past to fit the crime we suspect we are suspected of. By the time we reach home we have altered our history, discredited all alibis, documented and labeled evidence, and, opening the door, we begin to serve our sentence.

SUMMER

There is no breeze, sounds travel far in the dead air – I hear my friends the boxcars in the freightyard miles away. Nearer there is the monotonous whirr of sprinklers and the occasional soft purr of a passing car. The bland uneventfulness of such weather is oppressive because it seems to mirror exactly the emotions of a typical neighborhood. No conflict is apparent, no abrasiveness, and there is a direct continuity between the quiet, the lack of wind, the heavy summer air, and the souls of the gentlefolk hereabouts. There is no way out – no tunnels exist, no forged passports, no swift dashes for the border. Such calm conceals a deep despair that generates, the way a pond generates insects, the distant gunshot or scream that breaks the silence of so many summer evenings in American cities.

THE GHOST ON THE SECOND FLOOR

Children hear him upstairs near the rooms where they sleep. He lies there all day like a dirty sheet or a cloud— one with a face and a voice like an air conditioner, a mutterer, hard to understand. He makes lights go out. He murders small animals, stuffs them with cereal, and uses the buttons from pyjamas for their eyes.

GOLF

Though they seem carefree and childlike, golfers are, in fact, very sinister. Their ease and playfulness is merely a cover-up, a very clever one, for their darker aims. You may have noticed that newspapers occasionally print articles telling of people who have been injured or even killed by golf balls. Following such reports you will notice golfers grow restive and self-conscious. They are afraid they will be found out because the whole vast apparatus of golf has been developed to accomplish a single purpose: assassination.

JOY JOY

The day is saturated with tears. Old letters are illegible because of tears. Newspapers shred, wet with tears. The floor is slick, rugs float, all our saucepans overflow, windows and mirrors are stained with tears. They fall like snowflakes and hair. They pile up. The mailman drowns. Old ones rattle in boxes like cufflinks.

CHARLES BURCHFIELD

Pavement darkens with rain and then reaches that point when it suddenly brightens, catching light. Soon it reflects in the way a slow river gives back deep versions of the shore. Sidewalks become windows and we see strange lives in them — those remembered from other rainy afternoons when we walked home from school. The streets give off light from some other world. It taunts us with the life we meant to live, always dazzling and shimmering, full of intricate dances and unheard of songs.

THE PUBLIC LECTURE

No matter how good the speaker, the listeners always find him dull. A strange impatience makes its way through the room, a restlessness that shows itself in coughs and a nearly silent shifting of position. The uneasiness rises from the buried fact that this is a trial by ordeal. Far back in time the speaker lived only until he stopped talking; then he was quickly sacrificed and his flesh eaten by the audience. Not really aware of it, audiences today still wait restlessly for this climax—it shows itself most clearly when pauses occur, such silence is the audience's dis-ease—and the listeners are forced to dissipate their enormous feelings of frustration by slapping their hands together very hard when the speaker stops.

WHY I WROTE ON SIDEWALKS

All around me I saw people walking to semiannual dental appointments, their foreheads stamped *sane*. Each time I looked in their eyes I lost jobs, knowing they always slept eight hours and exercised every morning, making their bodies bullet-proof. Their winks blinded me. Their very presence involved me in scandals deeper than codes, and I knew that sinister, ink-stained thumbs were auditing my books. Their stares drummed me out of every corps I drew near, and this is why I wrote *How can I go on?* on all the sidewalks.

HOUSES & SHIPS

The houses are ships—run aground so long ago no one remembers—continually assailed by pirates. Because the times seem to have changed, the pirates now use disguises—their hooks and peglegs and big gold earrings are concealed by nondescript uniforms. But the boarding parties go on, made up of what seem to be paperboys, milkmen, and that ominous figure in gray who brings the mail.

BODIES

Given their natural inclinations toward betrayal, they cannot be trusted. They introduce foreign elements into our lives; they encourage appetites we exhaust ourselves resisting or satisfying; or they develop their own vices of the cells which we call disease. And since we have only their little hands to work with, we are helpless against them.

THESE PEOPLE

Who are all these people? You recognize them all, know their names and even parts of their secret histories. You have looked at their eyes and their teeth so often they seem part of the landscape around your hometown. But who are they? Tonight, sitting in a room with them, you watch as they peel like tangerines, change places, lose their way in the script, fumble, turn the faces of animals toward you, burn and freeze. Who are these people?

PROFESSORS

Many talk of dedication, service to youth and knowledge, scholarship and independent inquiry. This sort of talk is quite simply a ruse. Professors are voluptuaries of the dull, and the real masters are those who conduct themselves so cleverly that no one ever discovers that their dullness is, in fact, a brilliantly feigned act.

ON BEING NERVOUS

You rise to speak, confident, calm, certain of the impact of your wisdom—unwise courses will be altered, inane policies revised—but suddenly, as if a virus had hit you, you stammer, your thoughts cloud, you perspire, and, confused and embarrassed, you speak too quickly, badly garbling what you intended to say, apologize and sit down. What creates this effect? It is the change in altitude one experiences when rising from a sitting position.

FREE

Released from some task that was onerous and thus distasteful, we, for a time, inwardly gambol, feeling fresh air on the places where harness bit into our shoulders. Later, of course, fresh air proves oppressive and even the force of gravity a horrible imposition.

SETTLING DOWN

People are moving in up the street; the process of settling down begins. First the huge trucks come, then the smaller cartons in car trunks, and finally the people are inside, having gained entrance with their offerings. At short intervals their faces appear in the windows, like clowns dodging baseballs in a gallery, as they work with great energy putting up curtains and arranging furniture. Later, they make a great show of cutting and watering the lawn, dressed in carefully pressed old clothes. Their steps are springy, their faces open and alert for friendliness. There is a great pathos in all their earnestness and energy, this newfound excitement, this rediscovery of themselves. It is too familiar. We wonder how long it will take them to settle down like sediment and count weeds in their yard from old rockers on the porch.

CULTURE

Now, in late spring, the evenings are long and there is little to do. We sit a great deal, smoke and read stories chosen carefully for their dullness, the more predictable the better, and, though it takes great effort, converse in commonplaces and platitudes, admiring the weather as though it were a piece of jewelry. We are, of course, practicing an art no living creature other than man can cultivate. The name of this art is boredom.

HEROES!

Our efforts are heroic yet no one pays any attention. Look at our accomplishments. We throw off the heavy weight smothering us at dawn and get out of our beds! We shave! We dress! We lift spoonfuls of cereal to our lips! We open the terrible front door and step out fearlessly!

THE LONELY MAN

No one sees him standing beside the file studying his mail — all flyers, all third class. No one watches him in the lounge where he pretends to read trade journals, pages all blur and flutter. He is lonely this way all day. No one notices him as he eats slowly in the cafeteria, and though he even likes the food no one knows he does. Every day he is like a man wandering through a strange city looking for a place he can afford, but no room is cheap enough.

THE LONELY MAN SPEAKS

"Today I fly over roofs. I am a cloud with a purpose, an enormous Chinese kite with the fat cheeks of a fish. All afternoon I table-hop from building to building, chimney to chimney. I come home to each of you who waits so anxiously, to each of you I come back, and tell strange stories until you fall dreamlessly asleep, finally cared for as you were always meant to be."

THE LONELY MAN WRITES

"Dear—:
I carry cigarettes only because you may want one some day and my pockets are filled with matches, too. I sit in taverns for hours because some evening you may come in, decide to be a drunkard and want drinking companions with experience. I left the space at the top of this letter blank, of course, so that you may fill in your name."

THE AFFLICTION

The first rule: it must be kept secret. Even if only a hint is known, making it mysterious, leverage is lost. Minute signs of sympathy begin to edge into people's eyes which then begin to work on you like carpenter's tools hacking you into some grotesque shape and you become a monster without danger for them — in fact, an artifact that gives them pleasure. If the entire nature of the affliction is known, even the mystery dispelled, you are completely lost. You and your disease become one for a time; then you disappear into it, and, inevitably, people begin to call you by its name.

WE

We travel a great deal but are never welcome. Our bags disappear, conductors shunt us away from reserved seats, waiters and other officials look at our money as if it were stolen and at our faces as if they were those of terribly defeated candidates. Lateness becomes our way of life, but we are not hated, only distrusted the way men are who request small loans in order to gamble or buy cheap wine.

THE ORTHODOXY OF ROUTINE

We are told the age lacks faith, that no permanent values exist, that the world is unstable, but many, let us call them the heroes of punctuality, who would follow a dogma if it existed, have circumvented the problem by making of their routines, protocols, schedules, and agendas a watertight doctrine which they always adhere to, as they say, religiously.

DREAM REEL

We traveled all night. Clocks ticked us into places we had carved for sleep, scooped from snow with burning hands. Our fingers slept at their tips and our arms were limp as dolls' limbs. A camera whirred and we were at the usual whistle stop familiar from other nights, and immediately we tried to teach our eyes to look for jobs. In the lone hotel we saw the names of old friends reversed on blotters, and then they walked in the lobby, wearing their fathers' suits, faces unused as the pictures in high school annuals — still smiling as if they wore their biographies on sandwich boards: A STUDENT, A MIXER & AN ATHLETE. They told us this was the bottom of our dreams. Then the camera clicked and we felt ourselves roll up like shades, flattening out on strips of film. Our color faded, our voices were to our left, painted on the film. We reached out but could not touch them to shout ourselves awake.

DEMON

No matter how you shuffle your traits — making diligence and order turn up regularly — he is always there, waiting. In fact, the harder you try to hide him the more often he breaks into your nights like a party-crashing drunk spilling drinks, upending tables, yelling obscenities at ancient maidens. The trick, you see, is to admit him calmly, see that he is really you — not a double, but *you*, not some actor or black sheep but simply you. He fits your skin; take him places, feed him smoked oysters and good bourbon, let him dance any time he wants to, let him sing. If you fail to do this he will kill himself.

FRIDAY AT 4:30

Moons and pies sit around a table talking about their ingredients and chuckling over moon-jokes and pie-jokes. "Gooseberry" gets a big laugh. So many things happen! Adding machine unrolls a list of funny numbers while the sticky tongues of manila envelopes wag with pleasure. Test tube talks about urine samples and nudges syntax in the definition. They all chant, "Gracious! Oh gracious! Such fun!"

CONFERENCE

In the office you feel like a speared fish, the tines of office hours holding you in place no matter how much you struggle. There is the window, blue sky, and tree tops, but some sentry pads back and forth somewhere, and besides the escape committee would never approve your plan even if you found one among the typewriter keys. A figure enters and the interrogation begins—conducted so subtly there are no apparent questions, only small talk. But you notice slight changes—the interrogator is uneasy or blinks too often and then you realize this one is a prisoner too but somehow you have become the interrogator. No one has told you what to ask. The small talk goes on for a long time.

O TANNENBAUM

The Christmas season come, the time of giving, the wife enjoyed giving things to others. "It hurts them and makes me laugh," she said. But finally everything was bought and wrapped. "A profound sadness is on me," she said to the husband. "Have a crust of bread, sweet thing," he said. "Oh no, you need it. It's old and hard the way you like it," she said. Then she had an idea. "Since you are so tired why don't you stand still and be the Christmas tree? You can sit down on New Year's Day," she said. "O.K." he said. So he stood in a corner, much admired by uncles and aunts, though they wondered aloud when he would go back to work. Finally his needles got tinder dry and the wife threw him out.

THE ART OF THE WOODCUT

There is a great deal to be learned about conduct from this art. First, a decisive thing is done to an unblemished surface, the tool makes a clear deep line, and because of its general similarity to a pencil line the amateur often thinks of the work as a drawing until the print is made. Then he learns that the whole flat untouched surface is what is really like a pencil, strange and blunt to be sure, and that, further, everything has come out backwards.

THINGS

There is in things a silent insistence we usually manage to ignore. There are, for example, the long cold rails carrying trains or lying still during the coldest nights of the longest winters.

KILLING TIME

In the wake of the windstorm the park where the old men sit looks ruthlessly weeded. Trees pulled up, sidewalks split, benches out of line. But the palsied newspapers and cards are intact, checkers still click across the boards, and among the players there remains the strangeness of old men with boys' names, names that refuse to age: Jerry, Delbert, Tim. A few of them lean against the uprooted trees that left huge divots in the lawn, at home with the fallen. Soon riptooth and chainsaw will dice the trunks to fireplace size, but now they are just fallen timber for a while. I walk through the park, and then, unaccountably, browse in the second-hand bookstore where the unread novels sleep.

THE VISITOR

He times his arrivals perfectly, always coming in when you least expect him. Then he leaves so quietly you are left in mid-phrase, bewildered at finding yourself talking to an empty chair. Sometimes, too, he is just around—sitting in the study, say—and you are aware of it only because of an uneasiness which keeps you out of the study. He is very swift and very quiet and without any trace of the joviality everyone expects from such heavy, avuncular men. He comes and goes. He terrifies you because though he is your oldest friend you do not know his name.

THE TALENT HUNT

Stooges wait everywhere on high stools like tennis judges. They stake out spots in all the drugstores looking for blondes or hang around schoolyards and bus stations. They listen a lot and nourish themselves with mint-flavored toothpicks. At the same time the talent waits in lobbies smoking three packs a day, tans fading, skills going stale — pawned, withering in guitar cases. Busboys and carhops, the talent bends whichever way it's asked, giving it away, looking for *the big break.*

SIGNATURE

We write it often—our pens have memorized its contours and lines, our fingers are intimate with the complexities of loops and dots, we know this little drawing better than our wives. Yet when signing a check why are we nervous? Why do we feel that someone, *The One Who Knows*, will suddenly lean his padded shoulder across the counter menacingly and accuse us of forgery? And why do we know that we will, of course, be found guilty?

DOUBLE

There is a man, I know him only slightly, who sits in my chair, wears my face and clothes, in fact a perfect replica. He is called *The Citizen*. In reality he is a puppet I control. When he speaks no one sees my lips move.

MISSING

We read something we like very much but then it ends and no matter how often we thumb through the book we never find unread pages. We have truly read it all, consumed it entirely, and in our passion memorized every word, yet it still exists as it was when we first picked it up—unchanged—and we, too, are unchanged.

REPORT ON THE DAY

As usual there were too many mouths, too many noses and eyes. There was hair too and fragmentary visions of ears. But, as if to atone for this vulgar show of abundance, there was a great deal of silence. It seemed the answer to all questions, like this: *question . . . silence.* There were also the more complicated events: eyes turning away, a rare smile saying *If the world were only different we would love each other forever,* heads bobbing like dolphins, cold water from fountains, letters (one from an old enemy gently pouring salt in the wound of memory), meetings of strange snorting creatures in business suits, and the drive through the dark with all the traffic lights green.

CAVE

The evening is a cave. You wander through it, lost but for a faint glimmer of light, a tiny bulb turned on and off, up ahead. You pursue the glimmer through the slowest hours, your chair often moving at great speed, but the light always blinks off as you get near it. It is like a single phosphorescent fish scale or the smallest dime in the world and it is always out of reach. Even after the crucial hours have passed — nine, ten, eleven — and you are in bed, you still wander in the cave, searching all night for that tiny brilliant coin spinning just ahead of you.

THEY

They begin by speaking softly to us, saying, "Slow down a bit." Or, "Go outside if you want to do that." They are very calm, very kind, sitting quietly in their chairs and drinking coffee from their special cups. Soon, though, they begin to shout, "Don't! Don't! Don't!" Louder and louder and we become confused and run toward them for comfort, turn away in pain, spin in circles toward dizziness — "Stop! Stop that!" — in our confusion. What are we to do? We have been asking them all our lives, every day, day after day. Will this ever end?

FRIENDS

We ride this train together, pleased with the slow way time passes, but then tracks and ties warp, cars uncouple at random and nose into sidings in a manner that seems an open example of cowardice. People get off and on and sometimes we discover too late that the person we liked best was either a road agent or a Pinkerton man. This gives us a helpless feeling like spilling three drinks in a row. (Is getting drunk really worth it?) We amble on though as the train keeps dividing itself into segments and suddenly know that all that talk last night was just talk. We will never see those people again except in court, perhaps, or possibly at the far end of some other club car laughing with their true friends.

EGO LIVES ALONE

Your population may explode but mine dwindles until I breathe desert, think desert and acres of minus numbers; for me whole vacant townships wait to be filled in like answers. But when that has gone on long enough I begin to work by laboriously clearing and leveling the land, putting in water and electricity with numb fingers, laying out streets with my old warped ruler, and building thousands of small efficient houses quickly and cheaply so that I can then bring in the settlers and be their king.

A GATHERING

Midway through an evening the room divides itself. Continents spring up, whole drab new solar systems swing into view, and at that moment you know you have no membership anywhere, doomed to carry the luggage of irony alone across these trivial vast spaces forever.

KILLERS

You flinch at their cold eyes on dust jackets or across waiting rooms tapping their feet impatiently and staring as you try to sit quietly, only cradling your magazine, never reading, never even daring to flutter the pages. True professionals, they never smile as they sell you bus tickets and breath mints, counting out your change like bullets.

THE HARMFUL STATE

Nearly everything you see inspires suspicion. Little signals speak of the ominous future the world has in store for you. But this is only the condition of optimum health, indicating that, like a cat, you are wary. Such a state cannot harm you. The harmful thing is not to suspect, but to know.